Pieces of Me
Volume 2

Cecelia Green Jerrell

Published by:
Cecelia Green Jerrell
Bronx, New York

Book Cover: Lakeya Johnson,
Creative Revolution Media

Editing: The Self Publishing Maven,
Robin Devonish Scott

ISBN 13: 978-0990954019

ISBN 10: 0990954013

Bronx, New York .

Printed in the United States

Dedication

To my mother,
Ruth Green,
for the courage and strength she passed on–
I'm thankful!

Contents

Thank You

I cried out in misery, I was in agony, I was tortured, I cried out for deliverance, You tended to me, You ministered to me, You revived me and invigorated me

Thank You

I am renewed, I am whole, I am filled with gratitude, infused with love and appreciation, for concern and compassion were shown me in my tormented times of necessitude

THANK YOU

With God

I never walk alone

SOMEONE

so special

is always at my side

This

SOMEONE,

my very special guide,

helps me walk

a very straight stride

as I

ask, pray,

and sometimes cry

With GOD

comes truth

I can readily abide

With GOD

there is no need to hide

I never walk alone

GOD

is always right at my side

Peace Be With You

Did you set this as top priority?

Were you there in all ways-

physically, emotionally, mentally?

Were you attentive to obvious and subtle needs?

Were you supportive?

And, sincere?

Did you do the best you could?

Did you pray and put everything in God's care?

Then,

your best you did...

At

Peace,

Be

A Marvelous Day

May this be a day

that I

show compassion, give generously

reflect, pray and

give thanks for all of God's blessings

Just Like You

It's just like you
to be available
before even I knew
I needed you

It's just like you
to know what
I want to hear
even before I knew

It's just like you to reach for me
before I even knew
I desired you

It's just like you to see my strength
in everything I do
before I even knew

It's just like you to know exactly

what makes me

very happily coo

It's just like you to be you-

the perfect one for me-you

Love Came to Me

Love came to me

Love called me

I was not looking for it

I was not expecting it

But, when love appeared,

I cheered

I jumped for joy

I certainly was not coy

Love came to me

Love called me

It slipped pass all my guards

Love seared my heart,

gave me a new start

Now, I am a part of another

We laugh until we almost cry,

watch the sun slowly rise,

sing songs as our love grows strong,

dance to our own beat

truly treasuring...

the love that came to be

Deal or No Deal

Deal?

Or, no deal?

I am the one to decide.

You are at my side—deal.

But, you want an easy ride—no deal!

You invite me to the riverside—deal.

Yet, you sneak around and even hide—
no deal!

You say you will gladly provide—deal.

But, you feel your strict rules I must
abide—no deal!

You agree your wealth we will divide—
deal.

Yet, you very often lie—no deal!

You hear me when I confide--deal

But, you make remarks that are snide--
no deal!

You see all the times I try—deal

Yet, you behave like a brute outside—
no deal!

So, you want me to be your next bride—

"Absolutely not!" I cried

Our worlds do not coincide!

No deal, no deal, no deal!

Worry

Why must I worry?

Worry, worry, worry

Why do troublesome thoughts bombard
me?

And make me sick and weak?

Where can I seek relief?

How can I get it to stop?

What will banish it forever?

When will it cease?

Who can bring release?

Stop, think, believe!

Put everything in God's hands-

Feel the----

PEACE!

PEACE!

PEACE!

You Have, I Have

You have your life, I have my life

You see white, I see black

You say, "Half empty." I say, "Half full."

You hear, "No! I hear, "Yes!"

You like to Salsa in clubs, I like to line
dance in class

You eat tofu for breakfast, I eat
jellybeans for lunch

You feel joy, I feel happy

You have your life, I have mine

Although we are different,

We are content

You are, I am

Living in
A State of Love

Living

in

a

state

of

LOVE

I hear you whispering gently my name

I see you smiling warmly as I approach

I touch your cheek lovingly when I reach
you

I taste joy

I am happy

I feel desired, connected, whole

We

are

living

in

a

state

of

LOVE

I am your treasure

You are my gem

We are LOVE

Gifted Smile

Your smile

warms me

makes me smile

and giggle and laugh and laugh

and jump for joy, dance a jig,

and wiggle, jiggle and sizzle

I sparkle and marvel

Your smile is my gift

I know I am adored,

I am special, cherished, more

Your gifted smile

makes me feel like

one in a million

Unexpected Destination

I cruised to the Bahamas with a friend

It was a good time to relax and mend

I do believe we were starting a trend

The multitude of activities and classes to attend

Tickled our fancies and propelled us to grin

Soon we were browsing and just had to spend

Meeting, greeting we even found lost kin

Gambling night and day, we managed to win

Taking pen to paper, cards we did send

Then salsa dancing, injured my thin shin

Softly, so gently he caressed my chin

Truly, I acknowledged,

I was in Heaven

Let the Giving Begin

What are the best gifts?

How about time?

Walk with me, talk to me, tell me you
care

How about patience?

Wait for me quietly, give me extra time,
show me you care

How about empathy?

Feel my pain, find out why, see what
you can share

How about laughter?

Tell me a joke, play a game for two,
have fun if you dare

How about peace?

Speak to me softly, enjoy my silence,
tenderly touch my hair

Hold me

Hug me

Kiss me

Then, I'll know you do really care

Hope: A True Possibility

I yearn for reunification

Is it possible?

Or, is it too late?

I want to return to a happier time

I long for a relationship revival

I hope we can again be close

I hope we can renew our bond

I hope we can put right what went
horribly wrong

I hope...

I hope...

I hope...

Loss: A Treasured Relationship

We grew up together
We played, we cried
We baked, we fried

Oh, many things we shared
We helped each other
We cared for another

You gave me ice cream, I gave you
candy
You watched over me, I helped you
You wiped my tears, I rubbed your back
You prayed for me, I prayed for you

I trusted you, but you deceived me
I loved you, but you hurt me
I cared about you, but you cursed me

I am in pain

I ache

I am desolate

Our relationship is lost.

A Marriage Masterpiece

Luxurious, luminous, lasting love

Sweet, sweet love

It's all in the details

Ready!

Set!

Go!

Focus with a purpose,

Value time together

Maintain a caring balance

Romance and treasure one another

Pray for guidance

Add that extra heartfelt touch

Celebrate all that enhances the
two of you

Treasure the ultimate journey of love to
endless peace and joy

STAY STAY STAY STAY STAY STAY STAY
STAY STAY STAY

Make it always a perfect fit---

A Marriage Masterpiece

Is This Love?

a sure smile?

loads of laughter?

a tickled cheek?

a private wink?

a head resting on a shoulder?

gently touching fingers?

a soft knee pat?

listening attentively to a complaint?

talking it out calmly?

the "look"?

a moonlit walk on the beach?

Highlight of My Life

Are you the highlight of my life?

Do you want me as your wife?

Do you bring a happy, sincere smile to my face?

Can I hardly wait to see you in my space?

Who will plead your case?

Have you started the chase?

Will you make it pass first base?

Do you make my heart flutter and race?

Do you treat me with genuine grace?

Should I bring out my gown of lace?

Hope this isn't--

a complete waste!

I Could Have Avoided

I could have avoided all that trouble, all that trouble

If I had just remembered-hardening of the arteries, hardening of the arteries

I could have avoided all that trouble, all that trouble

If I had just remembered to keep my mouth shut, keep my mouth shut

and

hardening of the arteries, hardening of the arteries

But, no,

I had to

EXPRESS MYSELF, EXPRESS MYSELF!

In my life, at this time and age,

I don't want to be stifled, I don't want to be stifled

I WANT TO EXPRESS MYSELF, I WANT TO EXPRESS MYSELF!

But, should I?

According to a recent study, a wife who argues with hubby, increases her rate of—hardening of the arteries, hardening of the arteries

So, should I forgo saying:

"Well, actually, what I think…" or

"Seriously, wouldn't it be much better…" or

"That's not what I said…" or

"I don't agree with you…"

Or, should I remember:

Hardening of the arteries, hardening of the arteries?

Time With a Friend

Today was lovely

I shared it with a friend

One I've known since high school

But little time with I've spent

We made up for lost time

Drank water with lime

Walked in the park, talked about real
life

And what brings us delight

It was a time of reconnecting,

finding similarities and disparities

a day discovering

what makes each of us tick

Today was so lovely

I spent it with an old friend

*Time passed too quickly so
we must do it again*

*Sooner rather than later will be
our new trend*

Today will be treasured

For I shared it with a very dear friend

Always Available

Always available you are

At the ready I find you

In reach all the time

You are present for me

Whenever I am in need, I know you are
at hand,

Accessible for my every want, my every
urgency, my every crisis,

Always available you are, providing
guidance, insight, security, comfort

Paths to answers, solutions, and peace
are mine

Having you always available makes me
strong, stronger, strongest-

just as I need to be

Having you always available is best for
me, absolutely

Tell me, will this always be?

Appreciate You

I appreciate you

Really I do

You surely make me coo

It is definitely true

Who would have thought this

of big strong you?

You are the glue that keeps me new,

refreshed and on cue

There are very, very few people like
darling

you

Woe is Me

We clicked

and

connected,

We hugged

and

projected

Wow,

how ecstatic were we...

Too soon,

way too soon,

we collided

and disconnected

We slugged

And

felt rejected

How sad...

how very, very sad

were we to be...

Take Some Time

Take some time

you did today--

to open your home

prepare sustenance

be with friends

Take some time

you did today--

to welcome us warmly

foster good spirit

provide a venue for laughter

Take some time

you did today—

to listen to unforgettable remembrances

voice your own stories

recall experiences of our past

Today, you took some time—

you

brought joy

touched our hearts

promoted new memories

You took time

to be a friend, a really good one

You took time and

Thankful am I that you did

And Then I Smiled

You spotted me that summer day

Couldn't keep your eyes away

I caught your immediate attention

You felt the heat, the tension

I was window shopping,

not thinking of stopping

What you saw, you did like

Knew you had to quickly strike

Moved close,

wouldn't let me out of your sight,

caressed my arm, said,

"Honey, I won't bite, only woo you tonight."

I was window shopping,

not thinking of stopping

But, what I saw I did like

Knew I, too, had to strike

So,

I stopped,

turned and

profiled

And, then,

I smiled

We Laughed

Laughed we did,

today

way down deep

filling all

the nooks and crannies

that were

closed in defeat

crushed in sadness

drowned in despair

Loud was our laughter, today

riotous, infectious

Our laughter

flooded

our hearts

our minds

Joy now overflows

because we laughed today

Our laughs felt good

way down deep

We really laughed

today

Ha Ha Ha Ha

Fine and Elegant

You appear before me

poised and pure

so absolutely sure

demonstrating style and dignity

I am mesmerized

disoriented, more

fine and elegant, you truly are

I see

strength,

sophistication

My,

you are an enchanting star--

the very best,

I've seen so far

Fine and elegant,

You definitely are

Soothe My Spirit

I listen to soft, caressing words
words that fill me,
overflowing me with
joy, rightness,
nourishing me,

I am empowered

My spirit is soothed
I am alive, whole, rearing to go
I'm on my good foot,
ready to do it all
for
my spirit is soothed

You Influence Me

Influence me, You do

Naturally nourishing me

Forcing me to think clearly and

Live life to its fullest degree

Under your watchful tutelage

Everything

Neatly fits together for good, helping
me to

Control myself and my circumstances

Effectively leading me to make daring,
deliberate decisions that delight me

Evidence of My Journey

Spiritual Peace

Relaxed Mind

Happy Heart

Creative Spirit

Sound Healing

Emotional Well-Being

High Expectations

Real Results

Loving Acceptance

Therapeutic Cleansing

Ultimate Freedom

Life-changing Insight

Enlightenment

Empowerment

Openess to Ecstacy

Rediscovery of My

True Voice and Authentic Self

God

Thank You, thank You

I do thank You so much

I feel blessed

when

I'm driving on the road with

mad drivers all around me

when

I'm riding an elevator and it begins

to rumble and grumble

when

I'm making important decisions

and I'm not sure what to do

when

sitting on a train

and see confrontations getting
out of hand

when

I'm listening to someone

and not hearing what's intended

when

I'm feeling afraid

and not sure of the next step

For You sweep me up in Your cloak of
protection

and I am safe

You

Enveloped in Your warmth I feel comfort
You bathe me in Your everlasting love
enabling me to have faith and fidelity
You are my shepherd I accept Your
authority I accept Your authority You
guide me I see the light You enlighten
me You enlighten me I know what is
right You complete me I have it all I am
a true believer blessed and devoted to

You

To

You

Wondrous

Hoping for,

wishing for,

praying for

the most wonderful of all things in
married life—

to be free from unnecessary, ridiculous,
draining strife,

as a wife,

a most wondrous thing

in life

Fired Up

Fired up

Rearing to go

I'm ready to put on my show

Look at me

What do you see?

What do you think?

Will I deliver?

Do you see me aquiver?

Look at me-collected, calm, cool

Surely, no fool

Fired up

Rearing to go

Standing tall

Strong

Feeling like gold, if truth be told

I'm fired up, I'm fired up!

More than ready for this road

A hot tamale, I am

Bold

Fired up, fired up!

Be a Smile

Be a smile
SMILE

Forget old hurts

Let them go
SMILE

Believe in forgiveness,

It's worth your while
SMILE

Believe in change

People certainly do
SMILE

Brighten your life

And others' too
SMILE

Awaken joy

Banish strife
SMILE

Simply, be a SMILE

Love Needs Expression

Love needs expression
Hold me tightly,
tightly hold me
Listen to me carefully,
carefully listen to me
Hear my words clearly,
clearly hear me
Whisper softly in my ear,
in my ear, softly whisper
Caress me gently with loving hands
with loving hands, gently caress me
See into my heart
See into my heart
Love me truly
In me, look for good only
With me, share truthfully
Express your love for me
Express your love for me
Express it
Express it
Express it

Over the Moon

I'm over the moon
for you
You take me there
you really do
One look from your
warm, twinkling eyes
stirs my fancy,
makes me see stars,
has me yearning for caresses,
and long delicious kisses,
excites me so completely,
kindles sparks of desire,
sets me on fire,
arouses me
leaves me loving you
more and
more and more
and more
I'm over the moon for you

Real World, Back To

It's time

to return

return to the

real world

world of responsibilities sharing space-
physical, mental-being accountable
being there for others fulfilling needs
doing it someone else's ways-
stress

On hold, I must put myself, in the real
world

Leaving

I'm leaving

It's time to go

I'm moving on

It's past time to exit

I'm making my escape

It's out the door for me

It's departure time

I'm going away

I'm on the run

This is my exodus

I won't be back I won't return I LEFT

GONE!

GONE!

GONE!

Rough Road

Bumpy, rough road, hard to traverse,
bouncing me

up and down, round and round

My thoughts a jumble, afraid to tumble,
no time to fumble,

will not stumble

Bumpy, burdensome road, you will not
be the demise of me

worn, torn but not defeated, focusing
on being better treated

Seeing my way through the dark, feeling
like leaving my mark, I'm revved up, soul
ignited

I'm no wimp, certainly no fool, this just a
crimp in what I must do-stand up, speak
out, do what it takes, keep it moving,
seal it with a shout

Bamboozled and banished, you are

Deterred, I am not

Determined, I am

It is survival of the fittest

No bumpy, rough road can take me
down

I am tough, I will be around

Made in the USA
San Bernardino, CA
14 November 2014